picasso's goat

picasso's goat

joan cofrancesco

authorHOUSE®

AuthorHouse™ LLC
1663 Liberty Drive
Bloomington, IN 47403
www.authorhouse.com
Phone: 1-800-839-8640

Published by AuthorHouse   07/09/2014

ISBN: 978-1-4969-2536-7 (sc)
ISBN: 978-1-4969-2535-0 (e)

how can the cat sleep
the way
these ancient pipes bang!

i love to
massage yr feet
by the goat
in the garden

comfy

wood for the fire
beans in the cupboard
litter for the cat
windchimes
on my porch
futon affections

italia fest
beer
dancing
beer
accordions
more dancing
more beer

play with my hair
you say

your long brown
silky hair

glides thru my fingers
i hope beauty is truth

ufo's hover
over my basketball games
bathtub
barking dogs
bars
and parking meters—
which of the greek gods
are near?

poem to dlugos

slipping thru
the syracuse streets
i wish i owned
a pair of uggs
with fur inside
or that i was
in bed again with sue smith

on my desk
the branch will not break
69 unfinished poems
a photo
of a woman
holding a fish
she just reeled in

from barcelona
allen wrote jack he spent
another day goofing around
ate huge paella meal
and saw more museums—

on long island
jack and his mama
poured another drink

synergies among
pregnant women
ufo's
clocks
televisions
men with
dog heads
crawling babies
the world
trade center
as two
phalluses
keith
haring

tonight i wake with your
head on my shoulder, thick

brown hair i sink
my teeth into. sheets

full of cats.
your breath calms me

i squeeze tighter
i love my desire

for e.h.

at a typewriter
and bleeding

but perhaps not enough
and perhaps the wrong blood type

papa whose papa
kilt himself in michigan

double-barreled
12-gauge shotgun papa

papa whiskey wars & women genius
brains splattered all over the wall

i love the way your rack
sits on my bookshelf

i sit on
spanish steps
in rome
eating a gelato
leaning against
john keats
home

lighting the tree
in hanover square
six hundred colored bulbs—
i think of medieval monks
laboring in the monastery
on the illuminated manuscripts

allen took off with peter
spain italy austria
mosques museums monks
food and conversation
it's not what they saw
it's that they saw together

i am walking
under streetlights
a woman in a window reads
lesbos poetry
looks down at me
and smiles

a gentle good night
to you dylan
sipping in the white horse tavern
fern hill
coming back to you

waiting room

"The heart, which is the bastion of life, is also the repository of the past."
　　　　David Krafchow KABBALISTIC TAROT

rainy and dark out
i'm in the waiting room
listening to mozart
on my i pod
surrounded by worriers
Time in my lap

*

they are taking the vein
the saphenous vein
they will use it
to make a detour
around the blocked area
in the artery

*

the heart beats 72 times a minute, 100,000 times a day,
36,000,000 times a year and 2.5 billion
times during a lifetime

*

the depression
wwII
hiroshma
rat teeth

*

then rebuilding america
chrysler aged you
but
you continued to hum

*

a quadriplegic
talks to a nurse
about iraq

another man
wearing a yankees cap
reminds me of my father
coming home from work

he puts on his ny cap
goes to his garden
feeds the rabbits
sharpens his tools

*

in 1616 william harvey discovered the circulatory system

*

they call me
to say
the operation has started
a stainless steel
saber saw buzzes
in the background

i imagine you
floating above
the stretcher
one of chagall's lovers
watching them open
your chest

*

unlike prufrock
you never thought
you were missing anything
depression
wwII
you walked through life
eating the fattest peaches
and snickering at the eternal footman
and now you lie
etherized upon the table
*

on the grass
scribbling in my journal

cows
dad's pickup
& john deere tractor

slanted roof
i throw my ball onto

10 years old
silver dollar
in my pocket

mom watching me
from the window

*

*every day the heart creates enough energy to drive 20 miles,
and a lifetime is equal to driving
to the moon and back*

*

they call me to say
he is on bypass

*

my father protected
his garlic
from winter
buried his fig trees
in the ground
til spring

wrapped flower beds
in burlap and twine
came into the house
every summer
arms full of tomatoes
and aglio
for my mother's sauce

*

*early egyptians believed that the heart and other major organs
had wills of their own and would move around inside the
body*

*

they call again
they are coming off
bypass
his heart will
start pumping on its own
sometimes they have trouble
coming off

*

we rode
through the night
listening to
a.m.

neon jesus
on the metal dashboard

*

from you i learned
how to fish

and to love mickey & whitey

i sat at your feet
while you explained
what a pinch hitter was
and why they use different pitchers

i leaned back
in the clawed bathtub
safe
cause you were there

*

deer meat hardens
in the barn
the animal hangs
between the truck
and the lawn mower

*

the heart weighs 11 ounces, pumps 2,000 gallons of blood
through 60,000 miles of vessels
each day

*

like rilke's black panther
i pace the white halls
of the hospital

i catch glimpses of death
carrying a glass cane
decorated with skeletons and bones
he's in black scrubs
with a black designer surgical cap
he is all business

*

in the icu
bright lights
beeps
white sheets
my father
all connected
down to the finger
clipped to a monitor

*

*during an average lifetime the heart will pump nearly 1.5
million gallons of blood—enough to fill 200 train tank cars*

*

a nurse runs in
her pockets filled
with alcohol wipes
pens needles syringes

etc.
doctors follow
to remove the staples
and reopen the chest

*

the house
is how he left it
grey stucco
among apple trees
empty bird nests
in the gutters

in the fall wheat field
the old john deere rusts

*

a warm fire
a glass of merlot
song by satchmo—
ain't here long

car vs. jogger haiku

car vs. runner

doctor scribbling notes
in the emergency room
blood stained jogging pants

accident

i'm in the ER
sirens pagers monitors
what the hell happened?

blasting in OR
concerto in A minor
slicing to the beat

beeping monitors
staring at the ceiling light
pale under white sheets

reading poetry
by william carlos williams
the doctor poet

i can't seem to sleep
2 weeks in the hospital
i miss my own bed

roommate

i got scared to death
her hospital bed was empty
she's gone to x-ray

hearing the clock tick
watching penicillin drip
time passes slowly

like a prowling cat
illness came so silently
spring turned to winter

beside EKG
one hundred beats per minute
my heart gone amok

living on bedpans
lasix stops me from swelling
keeps me from drowning

no more attachments
to this material world
monitor's last beep

neuro-tangled brain haikus

"There is no subject whatever that is not fit for haiku."
--Basho

the new young interns
stiff in their white jackets
ready to control

screaming objections
patient doesn't want to take
his psychotropics

paranoia

nurse is dangerous
doctor is out to get me
the pills are poison

they wonder why i need ambien

clock ticks, nurse talk
vending machines keep humming
how can i sleep here?

manic state

aimless energy
like ulysses i wander
down the corridors

my doctor recommends a cat companion for menopause

sweat, worries, sleepless
2 a.m. cat on my head
doc, i think you're wrong

manic depression
lithium steadies my mood
no longer fatigued

i can hear the flutes
of Ur playing in my head
schizophrenia

the night before surgery

the sorrow of an old horse in a pasture
never running again. the plane that crashed into the towers
holds darkness in its wings for eternity.

each time van gogh touches his brush to the page
so many sunflowers and irises light up. perhaps that happens
because we have caused so much darkness.

each time a surgeon cuts through my skin
i hope he is like van gogh with a brush
though i know the universe can get along without me.

our bodies seem to remember our suffering
our hearts seem to clog like rusty drains
our souls remember all those smoky bars

last night i dreamt of
galloping beasts and dripping colors.
i was running in a field with a horse
no cares no suffering

how could it be that such suffering
could be shown by a sketch of
black crows flying through a dark cornfield?

a monkess
from tibet
i lite votive
candles

in the village
drinking coors lite
listening to patsy's
crazy
fingering a thin collection
of chinese poetry
a black cat rubs
against me

at the neue gallery
matare's *lurking cat*
catches my eye
i too would have been
degenerate
to the nazis

i rake leaves
my orange cat watches
from the window

drowsy from the heat
i wander into the garden
pick a ripe apple
and there you are again

let me always be
a young american girl
with a backpack
full of poems
and 200 euros
sipping ouzo
on a terrace
in greece
to the sound
of seagulls

incense
rises
reading
crow
by
hughes

amongst your poetry
art books
duke ellington
silk persian scarfs
let's have sake
and love our shadows

i love to watch her
take a bath
skylight sunshine
on her skin

i read george
seferis
my favorite waters
of dead sea

this eastern shit
ain't working

tai chi on saturday
meditation on sunday

drunk on monday
under a blue jean sky

breakfast

i am hypnotized
wind moving the pines
cats stretching

i sleep naked
at night
so i can dream of you—
i love to massage
your feet
by the goat
in the garden

the golden years before AIDS

"There is something massively forgetful about our contemporary moment, which avoids the years 1981-1997 and pretends that the world post-1997 is HIV-free.
                    --Richard Canning

the spirited
young men
outside
spiritus pizza
provincetown
the smell of
expensive colognes
mixed with sweat
everybody
leaving the bars
to get a slice
and a coke

fisherman's wharf
p-town t-shirts
suntan lotion
sunglasses
whale watch boats
2 lesbians
holding hands

rolling waves

hit the sand
sooth the pain
in our oz-like existence
we have
no thoughts
of tomorrow

21
looking out
the window of sam's apartment
summer of love
wandered down to
washington square park
then to times square
the guys went to
the bathhouses
i went to
gotham book mart

wandering through soho
in your
calvin klein black
tight jeans
and bomber leather jacket
and scarf
how devastating
you looked

nyc
1981
drank like piaf
loved like anais nin

i romanticized nyc
like isherwood
did berlin
it was
disco
art
stonewall
gays
then
AIDS

the kiss of death (love can kill you)

poppers
bathhouses
grace jones
all it took was one
glance
one nod
who would have guessed?

stonewall
gay pride
we came so far
then
AIDS

AIDS was like a black
panther lurking
around the disco floor
waiting to pounce
on my friends
and devour them

one by one

HIV test positive
dead blackbird
on porch

you looked so butch
in your das boot sneakers
when we went to see
al pacino in *cruising*
some say
you deserved it
being promiscuous
and after all
AIDS is
a punishment
from god

1981
ronnie turns his head away
and thousands die

1981
mysterious
gay cancer
night sweats
swollen lymph nodes
change in appetite
ks lesions
persistent cough
fever
people were
dying all around me

reagan didn't care
i felt like
i was living
in a B-movie
the heroine
fighting off
the mysterious
disease
from
mars

my cousin david
weak thin arms
he is hanging balloons
and disco ball
putting 1982 banner
across the wall
wondering if this is
the last time

in the ER
watching
a fly crawling
upside down
on the ceiling

panic
t-cell count
less
than 500

HZT
3TC

rattle that bottle
hope they work

rain

your watercolor rat
hangs above
my bed

let's stay in
and watch old
bette davis movies

we were reckless
wandered together
through nyc
rainbow flags
down 5th avenue
pride parades
bath houses bars
and now
you are lifeless
bedpan shining
in the sunlight

over his waterbed
hangs a crucifix
it is winter
but he is thinking
of summer
walking along the beach
with his lover
in p-town

summer 1980
a gentle breeze
blowing
soon he knows
all of this
and his memories too
will one day
be taken
from him

the experimental
drugs did not work
HIV
AZT
3TC
AIDS

in this
stainless steel
world
of bedpans
and forceps
i see a
person's
flesh

high cost of love

night sweats
gaunt cheeks—
was that one night
in barcelona
worth it?

you fucked
in the central park rambles
i warned you
but you said
"boys will be boys"

names project quilt

a patchquilt
of men who died
of AIDS
a succession
of names
fred jones 1960-1982
photographs, stars, angels
sheet music, rainbows,
hearts, letters, flowers
teddy bears, doves
mike smith 1955-1981
fabrics
ranging
from
satin
to canvas
a quilt made
to keep
you warm
at
night

we wore our
silence=death

t-shirts
as we walked
through the
streets
of
washington

mapplethorpe
keith haring
rudolph nureyev
michael bennett
isaac asimov
rock hudson
liberace
james merrill
anthony perkins
arthur ashe
freddy mercury
all the great
writers
artists
musicians
lost to AIDS
imagine
what we have
lost
from
their
deaths

time to flush
your heplock
take your

leucovorin
your cat purrs
beside you
on the bed
as you watch
your favorite
movie star
elizabeth taylor
in
cat on a hot tin roof

reagan couldn't
even say the
word AIDS
til rock hudson
appeared on tv

old blackbird
hops along your windowsill
"that bird keeps
smashing into my window"
he says "and wakes me up"
"maybe he is trying
to get in" i say
the bird flaps away
death will come soon
we both know it
but neither of us
will say
instead we watch
that old bird
and laugh
then you turn away

dizzy
lost again in
that strange
land

chest inflated
by a respirator
his mind in some
other dimension
tubes and needles
everywhere
there he lies
lungs clouded with
pneumocystis

you were once as happy
as a bottle of wine
with a 1913 vintage
then in came
the man with the scythe

mr. death
with his glass cane
filled with rainbows and skulls
he glides the sidewalks
i sit at my desk
listening to birds
outside my window
i stare at him
my fingers resting
on page 24 of
milton

today 321
is a dead patient
16 get well cards
on his nightstand

in the night corridor
of the VA
a nurse pushes
your stretcher
down to the morgue
je t'aime cousine adieu
god is sometimes cruel

christmas tree dying
christmas berries glowing
blood red
like memories

christmas
bells ring
he is come
but you are gone

plague

we were all afraid
nobody knew
where it came from
sunken face
purple blotches
i never kissed you
goodbye

my aunt sits
in silence and sews
a quilt for david:
vietnam vet
beloved son
i watch her hands weave
a music note
a black cat
a bright yellow sun
all the things he loved

i sit on
spanish steps
in rome
eating a gelato
what does john keats
have to do with this?

genius picasso
painted me
crazy lady with cats
before i was born

who is dlugos?
i seem to know that
before I understand
these words

no tv
pets or kids
and yet
i breathe

at the pompidou center

i'd trade
my black leather jacket
for that urinal
named mutt

35 years
at the marcellus
casket factory
i have quite
an imagination

Cream
in my ears
and all around
inside me

mama loves
a gianelli sausage
in a
hot italian roll

high with you
after a hot fudge sundae
the soft sax
of sanborn
your warm tongue
between my legs

sidewalks
covered with snow
i should shovel
but the cherrywood
fire glows and smells
almost as wonderful
as your soft skin
in my bed

simplicity

windows open
lilacs come in
siamese cat
purring beside me
haikus and love

prozac—
virginia
anne
and
sylvia still
alive

let's cuddle
under my cat quilt
we can
stack
wood
later

on my wall
baudelaire
degas's ballerinas
the woodstove
glows

after marie gitin

    syracuse
wires cross the blue spruces
    chipmunks and cat
round and round
      the steady rain

my cat
licking himself
on baudelaire

i am the drift
of the drunken boat
on its way
to luxembourg gardens

in a gay bar in new orleans
i saw tennessee williams drunk
eyeing young men—
cat on a hot tin roof

in jeans
white buddha t-shirts and
hoodies
we study
incense of i-ching
torah
each other

marmottan museum
imagination rockets
from lilypads

mist over the catskills
dew on our hiking boots

pont des arts
padlock on the bridge
marriage vows

i bought a new black
leather jacket
for $400
so i could look like
joan jett
instead i look
like somebody's secretary

i sleep
with dharma bums
beside my satin pillow

prowling
the metro
in paris
looking for ezra's petals

to lie
in bed all day with you
snow glistening
woodstove glowing

the smell
of sex
and incense
lingers longer
on my sheets
than you do

eating outside
at the bear
café
in woodstock
moonlight
in my
coffee

sundays
i am always ten
kneeling in st. mary's
reading my catechism
not understanding
transubstantiation

breakfast with kerouac
        after bruce hodder

drinking port wine
on the bed
cheerios in milk
ice on the window
one lone goose high up in the sky
heading for tibet

i know it
when I hear *jeep's blues* by
duke ellington
i know it
when i see
dekooning's yellow slash
across the canvas
i know it
when i touch
the eiffel tower
i know it
when i see
your breasts rising above
me naked
in my big blue water bed

janine gave me
a christopher medal
to slay
all the imaginary dragons
who fly with me
on airplanes

ménage a trios 1969

lava lamp
lace
feathers
leather
patchouli
abbey road
arms everywhere
who's touching who
who cares

rainy afternoon
we talk about
movies poetry
kierkegaard
cardiology
two childless women
one orange cat

it's the nyc
skyscrapers
against the moon
and i'm in
attendance

i sit at my desk
between six o'clock
and the planets
trying to figure out
why you left

on a train
from syracuse to nyc
my first love
my city lights pocket book
#19 *lunch poems*
in my leather jacket

with the artwork
of keith haring
and the poetry
of prevert
i make
my own calendar

listening to the couple
in the apartment below me
having sex
staring out at
my garden gnomes
covered with snow

gore vidal
never
came out
and at the end
had only a cat
in his bed
who died
6 months before
gore

colored lights
lasagna
johnny mathis
hot cider rum
furry snoopy ornament
on the tree

when i eat you
i taste
smoke grapes chianti
and know
where you came from

searching
for rimbaud's
tomb in
pere lachaise
cemetery
perhaps
it has
wandered away

the way my cat
stares at the fishbowl
you stare
at me